TRAINING SAM

This is Sam. Sam is a dog. He is a happy pet. I feed Sam when he is hungry. I play with Sam. I like Sam and Sam likes me. If I want Sam to be a good pet, I must train him.

First, I teach Sam to come. I put Sam on a long rope. Sam walks around, and is soon far away. I clap my hands, and say, "Sam, come!" Slowly, I pull the rope until Sam is with me. I do not pull hard. I do not want to hurt Sam. Every day I work with Sam. Now Sam comes when I call him.

Next, I teach Sam to walk on a leash. I hold most of the leash in my hand. I want Sam to learn to walk next to me. Gently, I tug on the leash and say, "Sam, walk!" Sam learns to walk next to me.

Last, I teach Sam to sit. I wave my hand down and say, "Sam, sit!" I gently push Sam down until he sits. Soon, Sam learns to sit.

I never hit Sam. I tell him when I am angry, and I pet him when he does well. I know that if I take good care of Sam, he will always be my friend.

QUESTIONS FOR TRAINING SAM

1. What is the name of the dog in the story?

   _____

   _____

2. What must the person do to make Sam a good pet?

   _____

   _____

3. What three things does Sam learn to do in the story?

   _____

   _____

4. What does the person do to Sam when he does well?

   _____

   _____

5. What does Sam learn <u>first</u>?

   _____

   _____

6. What does Sam learn <u>last</u>?

   _____

   _____

7. The story tells us that Sam likes the person in the story. Name two reasons why Sam likes the person.

   _____

   _____

8. Do you think it took one day to teach Sam to come, to walk on a leash, and to sit? Why do you think so?

   _____

   _____

9. The person in the story wants to teach Sam more. Name three other things she or he might teach Sam.

_____

_____

10. How does training a dog make it a good pet?

_____

_____

11. Write a title for the story. Use as few words as possible.

_____

_____

12. How is training a dog to come like training it to walk on a leash? How is it different?

_____

_____

13. In your own words, tell how to teach a dog to sit.

_____

_____

14. What would happen if the person teaching Sam yelled at the dog? Would Sam learn more quickly, or would he learn more slowly? Why do you think so?

_____

_____

15. The story says, "If I train Sam, he will be a good pet." Is this a fact, or is it an opinion? Why do you think this way?

_____

_____

16.

_____

_____

Name _____ Date _____

THE FROG

Look at the picture of a frog. A frog's body helps it to live in a pond.

A frog's skin is bumpy. The color of a frog can be green or brown. It looks like a rock when it sits still.

A frog has eyes on top of its head. It can sit under water, but keep its eyes above the water. The frog can see what is around it.

The back legs of a frog are very long. With strong back legs, the frog can jump far.

Look at the frog's back feet. There is skin going from toe to toe. The back feet help the frog swim.

Next time you see a frog, look at it carefully. Can you find other ways its body helps the frog to live in a pond?

QUESTIONS FOR THE FROG

1. What does a frog's body help it to do?

   _____

   _____

2. What makes a frog look like a rock?

   _____

   _____

3. What do the frog's back legs help it to do?

   _____

   _____

4. What helps the frog to swim?

   _____

   _____

5. What part of a frog does the story tell about first?

   _____

   _____

6. What part of a frog does the story tell about last?

   _____

   _____

7. The story tells us that the skin of a frog makes it look like a rock. How can this help a frog to live in a pond?

   _____

   _____

8. Look at the picture of the frog. Can you find another body part that helps the frog to live in a pond?

   _____

   _____

9. Would a frog be able to live in a dry, sandy desert? Why do you think so?

_____

_____

10. The story tells us that frogs sit under water, but they keep their eyes above the water. Why does a frog do this?

_____

_____

11. Write a title for the story. Use as few words as possible.

_____

_____

12. How are frogs and lizards alike? How are they different?

_____

_____

13. In your own words, tell how a frog's skin helps it to live in a pond.

_____

_____

14. Imagine a frog living in a pond. What would happen if the frog were bright red, not green or brown?

_____

_____

15. The story says, "With strong back legs, the frog can jump far." Is this a fact, or someone's opinion? How do you know?

_____

_____

16.

_____

_____

Name _____   Date _____

READING TRACKS

After it rains, look for bird tracks. Look in places where there is mud. Did you know that you can tell what kind of bird walked in the mud?

Most bird tracks look alike in many ways. Birds have three front toes and one back toe. The way a bird walks makes its tracks special.

Sparrows are hopping birds. They put both feet together. When they hop, they land on both feet. What do you think sparrow tracks look like?

Starlings are walking birds. They walk like people. They put one foot in front of the other. What do you think starling tracks look like?

Some birds, like robins, hop and walk. What do you think robin tracks look like?

Look at the picture of bird tracks. Were you right?

Look for pictures of other animal tracks. As you learn more, you will know what tracks frogs, turtles, ducks and even dinosaurs make.

QUESTIONS FOR READING TRACKS

1. Where is a good place to look for bird tracks?

    _____

    _____

2. How are most bird footprints <u>alike</u>?

    _____

    _____

3. What makes bird tracks special?

    _____

    _____

4. Name the three birds in the story.

    _____

    _____

5. Which bird tracks did you read about <u>first</u>?

    _____

    _____

6. Which bird tracks did you read about <u>last</u>?

    _____

    _____

7. People found dinosaur tracks in rocks. After reading this story, what is one thing you might learn about a dinosaur by looking at its tracks?

    _____

    _____

8. The story tells us to look for bird tracks after it rains. Why would a dry day be a bad time to look for tracks?

    _____

    _____

9. What might a robin's tracks look like just before it begins to fly? Next, draw a picture of what these tracks might look like.

_____

_____

10. Some people look for animal tracks as a hobby. A hobby is something you like to do when you are not working. Why do you think looking at animal tracks is fun for these people?

_____

_____

11. Write a title for the story. Use as few words as possible.

_____

_____

12. Look at the picture of bird tracks. How are the tracks of a sparrow like the tracks of a starling? How are the tracks different?

_____

_____

13. In your own words, tell about the tracks made by robins.

_____

_____

14. Imagine that a sparrow hurt one of its legs. Tell what its tracks might look like. Next, draw a picture of the tracks you might see.

_____

_____

15. The story says, "Every bird makes its own special tracks." Is this a fact, or someone's opinion? How do you know?

_____

_____

16.

_____

_____

Name _____ Date _____

IN THE DEEP SEA

People have seen all of the Earth. We have seen all the animals. We have walked on every spot of Earth. Is this true?

No, it is not true. No one has seen most of the animals in the sea. No one has walked on the deep sea floor.

Many people are looking in space to find new life. People called oceanographers look for new life right here on Earth. They look in the sea.

There is no light deep in the sea. The sun cannot reach deep under water. Nine out of ten animals in the deep sea shine. Some blink their lights on and off, like the angler fish with its shining string.

The gulper eel looks as if it could live only on Mars. Most of its body is a large, open mouth with many sharp teeth.

Someday oceanographers will live in the deep sea. Then they will look for more wonderful animals. Would you like to join them?

QUESTIONS FOR IN THE DEEP SEA

1. Have people seen all the animals on Earth?

   _____

   _____

2. Who looks in the sea for new life?

   _____

   _____

3. How many deep sea animals shine?

   _____

   _____

4. What does the gulper eel look like?

   _____

   _____

5. Name the first animal described in the story.

   _____

   _____

6. What will oceanographers do after they live in the deep sea?

   _____

   _____

7. Why is the deep sea eel called the gulper eel?

   _____

   _____

8. Do oceanographers think it is good to look for life in the deep sea? Why do you think so?

   _____

   _____

9. Will oceanographers always look for new animals? Why do you think so?

_____

_____

10. Why would someone want to be an oceanographer?

_____

_____

11. Write a title for the story. Use as few words as you can.

_____

_____

12. How are oceanographers and astronauts alike? How are they not alike?

_____

_____

13. Tell about the two animals in the story. Use as few words as you can.

_____

_____

14. How will people feel about the sea when oceanographers find new animals? Why do you think so?

_____

_____

15. The story said, "Someday oceanographers will live in the deep sea." Is this a fact? Why do you think so?

_____

_____

16.

_____

_____

Name _____   Date _____

"LITTLE PETER" THE CLOWN

Who was the first clown? The first clown worked for kings. His job was to make the king laugh. He did not look like the clowns we see today. He did not wear big clothes or paint his face.

The first clown to paint his face was from France. They called their clown Little Peter, or Pierrot.

Little Peter painted his face white. Even his clothes were white. His big clothes, pointed hat, and large buttons made him look like today's clowns.

Little Peter was a smart clown. He was also very sad. He painted his face white so no one could see his sad face.

The next time you see a clown, look at the way he or she dresses. Are the clown's clothes big? Does the clown paint his or her face? If the clown does, he or she is following in the steps of the sad clown, Little Peter.

QUESTIONS FOR "LITTLE PETER" THE CLOWN

1. For whom did the first clowns work?

   _____

   _____

2. Where was Little Peter from?

   _____

   _____

3. How did Little Peter feel?

   _____

   _____

4. What color were Little Peter's face and clothes?

   _____

   _____

5. Which clowns did the story tell about first?

   _____

   _____

6. Who was the first clown to paint his face?

   _____

   _____

7. What one word best tells about Little Peter?

   _____

   _____

8. Was Little Peter a good clown? Why do you think so?

   _____

   _____

9. Will clowns always dress in big clothes? Why do you think so?

_____

_____

10. Why did Little Peter want to paint his sad face?

_____

_____

11. Write a name for the story. Use only a few words.

_____

_____

12. How was Little Peter like today's clowns? How was he not like today's clowns?

_____

_____

13. In a few words, tell what Little Peter looked like.

_____

_____

14. How did Little Peter change the way clowns look?

_____

_____

15. The story said, "Little Peter painted his face white." Is this a fact? Why do you think so?

_____

_____

16.

_____

_____

MARY READ: LADY PIRATE

We think of pirates as men. On dark ships, men with peg legs are ready to fight.

Not all pirates were men. Some pirates were women. One of these lady pirates was Mary Read.

Mary ran away from home when she was 14. She ran away to sail the sea. One time she joined the army. Soon she went back to the sea she loved.

Mary Read became a pirate. She stole ships. She used a gun and knife. Next, she worked for countries at war. They asked Mary to steal their enemy's ships.

One day Mary met Anne Bonny. The two women worked together. They dressed like men and were as mean as any pirate.

In 1720, the Navy caught Mary and Anne. Mary Read died in prison from a fever. Anne Bonny disappeared. No one ever saw Anne again.

QUESTIONS FOR MARY READ: LADY PIRATE

1. Were all pirates men?

   _____

   _____

2. Name the two lady pirates in the story.

   _____

   _____

3. When did the Navy catch Mary Read?

   _____

   _____

4. How did Mary Read die?

   _____

   _____

5. What did Mary Read do before she was a pirate?

   _____

   _____

6. What happened to Mary after the Navy caught her?

   _____

   _____

7. What one word best tells about Mary Read?

   _____

   _____

8. Was Mary Read a friendly person? Why do you think she was or she wasn't?

   _____

   _____

9. Do you think Anne Bonny was a pirate after she disappeared? Why do you think so?

_____

_____

10. Why was Mary Read put in prison?

_____

_____

11. Write a title for the story. Use as few words as you can.

_____

_____

12. How was Mary Read like other pirates? How was she not like other pirates?

_____

_____

13. Tell about Mary Read's life in your own words.

_____

_____

14. How did Mary Read make people on other ships feel? Why do you think so?

_____

_____

15. The story said, "(Mary Read and Anne Bonny) were as mean as any pirate." Is this a fact or an opinion? Why do you think so?

_____

_____

16.

_____

_____

Name _____   Date _____

JOHN ROCK

John Rock was an American black man born before the Civil War. He lived in the North, so he was a free man. People with black skin in the South were slaves. They worked without pay, and could not go to school

John Rock was born in 1825. He stayed in school until he was 18 years old. John wanted to help people. At the age of 19, he became a teacher.

John Rock never stopped learning. He read about medicine. He tried to go to school to become a doctor. The school did not let him in. They did not let black people go to medical school.

John did not give up. He taught himself to be a dentist. He worked very hard to help people. John worked so hard he became sick. Still, he did not give up.

When John felt better, he studied law. In 1865, John Rock became the first black lawyer recognized by the Supreme Court.

Throughout his life, John Rock helped his fellow human beings. He died in 1866.

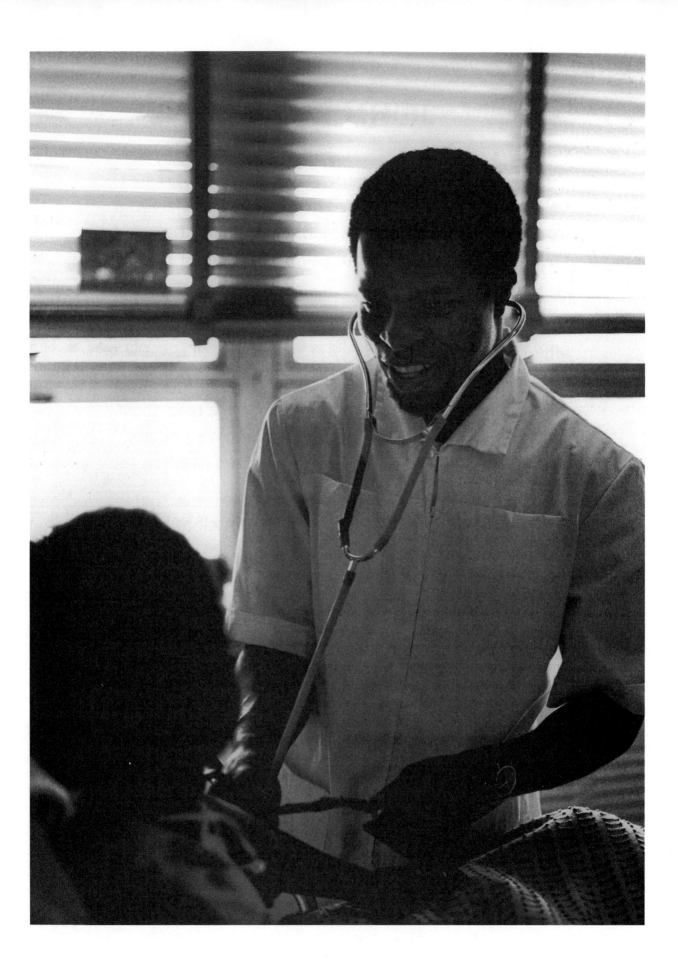

QUESTIONS FOR JOHN ROCK

1. In what year was John Rock born?

   _____

   _____

2. How old was John Rock when he became a teacher?

   _____

   _____

3. What kept John Rock from going to medical school?

   _____

   _____

4. In what year was John Rock recognized as a lawyer by the Supreme Court?

   _____

   _____

5. What was John Rock's first job?

   _____

   _____

6. What did John Rock become after he was told he could not go to medical school?

   _____

   _____

7. What one word do you think best describes John Rock?

   _____

   _____

8. Do you think that staying in school until the age of 18 helped John Rock become such a great man? Why do you think so?

   _____

   _____

9. John Rock understood that he needed to learn as much as he could to make his life important. He worked hard and never gave up.
What do you want to do when you finish school? What will you need to do to reach your goal?

_____

_____

10. Why do you think that John Rock kept working to make his dreams come true? Why do you think he did not give up?

_____

_____

11. Write a title that best describes this story. Use as few words as possible.

_____

_____

12. John Rock wanted to be a doctor. He became a dentist instead. How is a doctor like a dentist? How are they different?

_____

_____

13. In your own words, tell why John Rock never became a doctor.

_____

_____

14. After reading about John Rock, have your ideas about your future changed? How have they changed?

_____

_____

15. The story said, "Throughout his life, John Rock helped his fellow human beings." Is this a fact or an opinion? Why do you think so?

_____

_____

16.

_____

_____

Name _____   Date _____

BRER RABBIT AND ANANSI THE SPIDER

Brer Rabbit likes to play tricks. He plays tricks on his friends. You can read about Brer Rabbit in very old stories from Africa.

There are many African stories about small animals. These animals want all the food. They do not like to share. How do these small animals get what they want? They trick their friends.

Anansi the Spider also likes to play tricks. Anansi likes to eat. He likes to eat everything he can. The spider tries to trick his friends to get a lot of food. One day his trick did not work. Anansi lost all the hair on his head.

Brer Rabbit and Anansi stories are funny. They teach something, too. They tell you to be good to your friends.

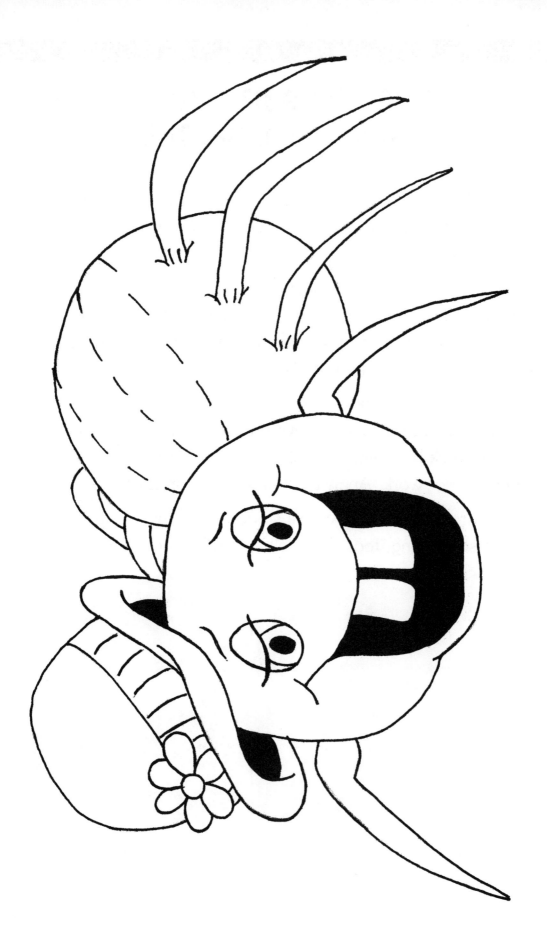

QUESTIONS FOR BRER RABBIT AND ANANSI THE SPIDER

1. Where do the Brer Rabbit stories come from?

   _____

   _____

2. How do Brer Rabbit and Anansi get what they want?

   _____

   _____

3. What does Anansi the Spider like to do?

   _____

   _____

4. What do Brer Rabbit and Anansi stories teach you?

   _____

   _____

5. What does Brer Rabbit do before he gets what he wants?

   _____

   _____

6. What does Anansi get after he tricks his friends?

   _____

   _____

7. What one word tells about Brer Rabbit?

   _____

   _____

8. Do you think people like Brer Rabbit and Anansi stories? Why do you think so?

   _____

   _____

9. Do you think people will tell Brer Rabbit and Anansi stories for a long time? Why do you think so?

_____

_____

10. Why did Brer Rabbit and Anansi use tricks to get what they wanted?

_____

_____

11. Write a title for this story. Use only a few words.

_____

_____

12. How are Brer Rabbit and Anansi alike? How are they not alike?

_____

_____

13. Tell how Anansi the Spider gets what he wants.

_____

_____

14. Anansi the Spider is very small. He tricks his friends to get what he wants. How would Anansi get what he wanted if he was a big lion?

_____

_____

15. The story says, "Brer Rabbit and Anansi stories are funny." Is this a fact or what someone thinks? Why do you think so?

_____

_____

16.

_____

_____

Name _____   Date _____

THE CALDECOTT MEDAL

Randolph Caldecott was born in 1846. Randolph walked in the woods when he was a little boy. He drew pictures of the animals. Randolph wanted to be an artist.

"Randolph should learn about money," his father said. "He needs a real job."

Randolph tried to make his father happy. When he grew up, he worked in a bank. Randolph was very sad. At night Randolph went to art school. He loved to draw pictures.

In 1875, Randolph Caldecott drew pictures for the book *Old Christmas*. Everyone liked his pictures. More people wanted his drawings in their books. Randolph drew many pictures for picture books.

In 1886, Randolph Caldecott died. He was only 40 years old. He was an artist for only ten years.

In 1939, people began to give prizes to the best picture book of the year. They called the prize the Caldecott Medal. Now we will always remember the joy and beauty Caldecott gave the children of the world.

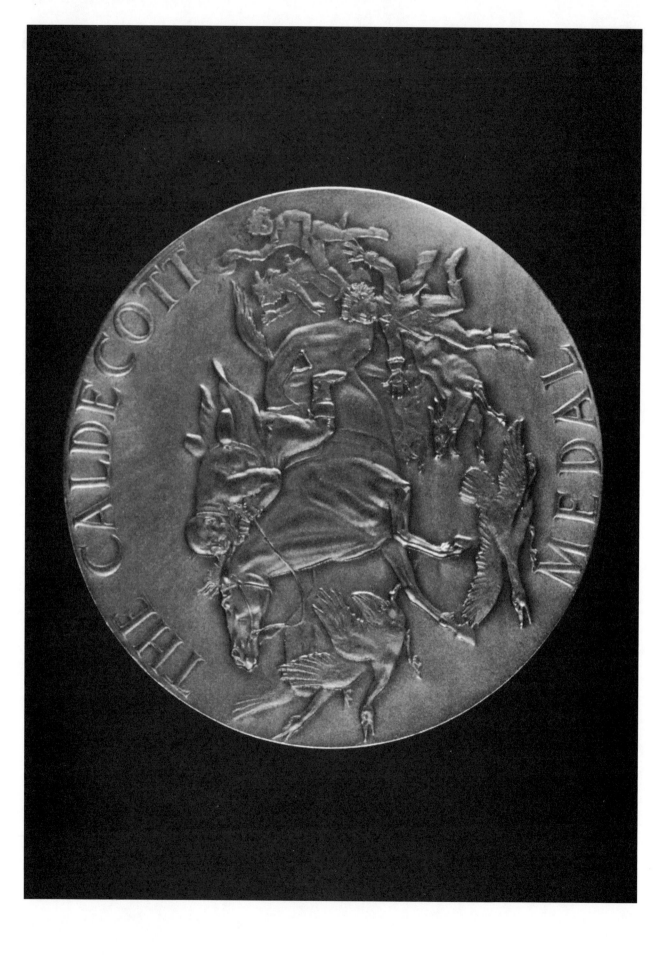

QUESTIONS FOR THE CALDECOTT MEDAL

1. When was Randolph Caldecott born?

   _____

   _____

2. Where did Randolph work when he grew up?

   _____

   _____

3. What book did Randolph Caldecott draw pictures for in 1875?

   _____

   _____

4. What is the name of the prize given to the best picture book of the year?

   _____

   _____

5. Where did Randolph Caldecott work before he drew the pictures for Old Christmas?

   _____

   _____

6. Which came first, the Caldecott Medal or Randolph Caldecott's death?

   _____

   _____

7. What one word best tells about Randolph Caldecott?

   _____

   _____

8. Why was Randolph Caldecott sad when he worked for a bank?

   _____

   _____

9. Look at several picture books printed this year. Which one do you think will win the Caldecott Medal? Ask your librarian to tell you if you were right.

_____

_____

10. Why was the prize for the best picture book named after Randolph Caldecott?

_____

_____

11. Write a title for this story. Use as few words as you can.

_____

_____

12. Look at a picture by Randolph Caldecott. Now look at pictures by Chris Van Allsburg. How are the pictures alike? How are they different?

_____

_____

13. In your own words, tell how Randolph Caldecott became a picture book artist.

_____

_____

14. How did Randolph Caldecott's father affect his life?

_____

_____

15. The story said, "He (Randolph Caldecott) was an artist for only ten years." Is this a fact or someone's opinion? How can you prove your answer?

_____

_____

16.

_____

_____

Name _____   Date _____

THE COLOR WHEEL

Painting is fun. You can paint a rainbow if you have many colors. You can make any color you want if you know how.

Painters make their own paint colors. They get just a few colors. Then they mix the paint to make the color they need.

If you need paint, you can just get red, blue, and yellow. Painters use color wheels to help them make colors.

Look at the color wheel. It tells you to mix red and blue to make purple. If you mix yellow and blue, you get green. What color do you make if you mix yellow and red?

With the colors red, blue, and yellow you can make any color you want. Someday your teacher will say, "You may have only three paint colors." What colors will you ask for?

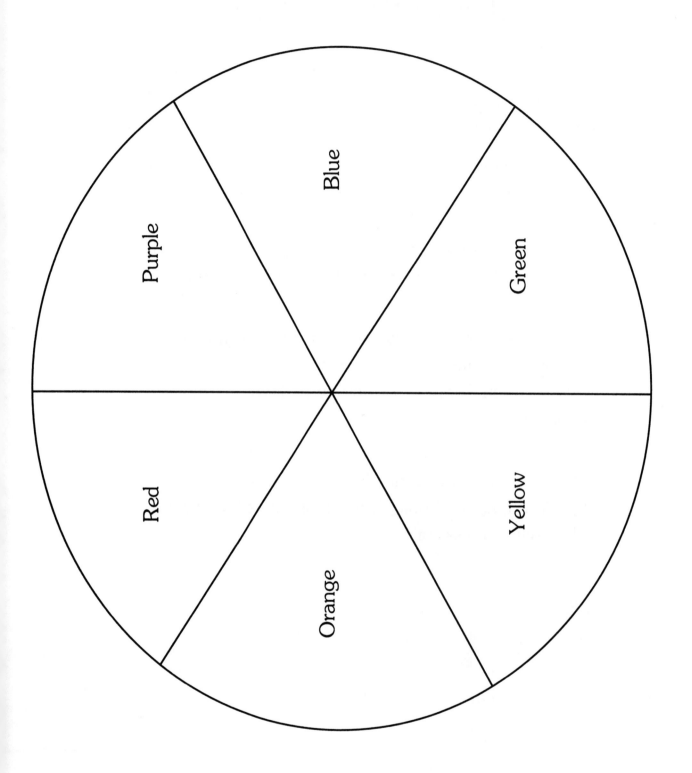

QUESTIONS FOR THE COLOR WHEEL

1. How do painters make the colors they need?

   _____

   _____

2. What three colors do you need to make any color you want?

   _____

   _____

3. Name the six colors on the color wheel.

   _____

   _____

4. What color will you get if you mix red and blue?

   _____

   _____

5. What is the first color the story teaches you to make?

   _____

   _____

6. What is the second color the story teaches you to make?

   _____

   _____

7. Why is the picture in the story called a color wheel?

   _____

   _____

8. Look at the color wheel. What two colors do you mix together to make orange?

   _____

   _____

9. Name one way you might use the color wheel to help you in the future.

_____

_____

10. Why might a painter want to mix her or his own colors?

_____

_____

11. Write a title for this story. Use as few words as possible.

_____

_____

12. Would you like to buy the color paint you need, or mix paint to make your own colors? Why do you feel this way?

_____

_____

13. In your own words, tell how you use the colors red, blue, and yellow to make three new colors.

_____

_____

14. After reading this story, will you change the way you use paints? Why do you think so?

_____

_____

15. The story tells you to mix red and blue paint to make purple. Is this a fact? How can you prove your answer?

_____

_____

16.

_____

_____

Name _____   Date _____

TO FLY OVER THE OCEAN

In 1927, planes did not fly far. The planes were small. They did not go fast.

Planes could not fly over the ocean. Charles Lindbergh wanted to be the first person to fly over the ocean.

On May 20, 1927, Lindbergh began to fly over the ocean. He had a very small plane. Lindbergh called his plane The Spirit of St. Louis.

Lindbergh could not see out the window. To see out, he looked in mirrors. He had one mirror to see behind him.

After 33 hours, he landed on the other side of the ocean. There were many parties. People were happy he flew over the ocean.

You can see his plane today. It is in a special place in Washington, D.C.

"Charles A. Lindbergh ... landed at Le Bourget Airport, Paris, at 5:24 this afternoon, thus becoming the first person to fly from New York to Paris nonstop."—Lowell Thomas, May 21, 1927

QUESTIONS FOR TO FLY OVER THE OCEAN

1. What did Charles Lindbergh do?

   _____

   _____

2. What did he call his plane?

   _____

   _____

3. On what day did Lindbergh begin to fly over the ocean?

   _____

   _____

4. How did Lindbergh see out of his plane?

   _____

   _____

5. What did people do after Lindbergh flew over the ocean?

   _____

   _____

6. How many planes flew over the ocean before May 20, 1927?

   _____

   _____

7. The story said, "People were happy Lindbergh flew over the ocean." Why do you think they were happy?

   _____

   _____

8. Reread the fourth paragraph. Do you think it was easy for Lindbergh to fly over the ocean? Why do you think so?

   _____

   _____

9. Will people always enjoy reading about the flight of Charles Lindbergh? Why do you think so?

_____

_____

10. Why did Charles Lindbergh want to fly over the ocean?
    Would you like to do something no one has done before? Why do you feel this way?

_____

_____

11. Write a title for the story. Use as few words as possible.

_____

_____

12. Look at a picture of The Spirit of Saint Louis. Look at a picture of a jet plane. How are the two planes alike? How are they different?

_____

_____

13. In your own words, tell about Charles Lindbergh's flight over the ocean.

_____

_____

14. Charles Lindbergh was the first person to fly across the ocean. How did his flight change the way people traveled around the world?

_____

_____

15. The story said, "People were happy he (Lindbergh) flew over the ocean." Is this a fact or someone's opinion? Why do you think so?

_____

_____

16.

_____

_____

Name _____   Date _____

SUPER-FAST TRAINS

When we think of trains, we think of slow trains rolling across the West. That picture of trains is changing, and it's changing fast!

In Japan and France, high-speed trains are racing across the land. They are so fast that people use trains, not planes.

New tracks help the trains move very fast. Turning tracks do not lie flat on the ground. They rise up on the outside, like race tracks for cars. The trains can turn without slowing down.

The Bullet Train of Japan runs up to 130 miles per hour. It runs on electric wires that are over the train.

France's trains can move people faster than an airplane. Their trains move up to 254 miles per hour. The fastest steam train can go only 126 miles per hour.

Someday trains will run in big tubes. Magnets will lift them off the ground. These speeders will move at over 745 miles per hour.

QUESTIONS FOR SUPER-FAST TRAINS

1. What is the name of Japan's fast train?

   _____

   _____

2. How fast does the Bullet Train run?

   _____

   _____

3. How fast does France's train move?

   _____

   _____

4. How fast can the fastest steam train go?

   _____

   _____

5. Which train does the story tell about first?

   _____

   _____

6. What is the second train the story tells about?

   _____

   _____

7. What one word best tells about the Bullet Train?

   _____

   _____

8. Do people want to ride on very fast trains? Why do you think so?

   _____

   _____

9. Will people make trains that go faster in the future? Why do you think so?

_____

_____

10. Why do Japan and France make such fast trains?

_____

_____

11. Write a name for the story. Use only a few words.

_____

_____

12. How is the Bullet Train of Japan like steam trains? How are they not alike?

_____

_____

13. In your own words, tell about the tracks used by super-fast trains.

_____

_____

14. How will a train that goes 745 miles in one hour change the way people go from place to place?

_____

_____

15. The story said, "The Bullet Train of Japan runs up to 130 miles per hour." Is this a fact or an opinion? How can you show you are right?

_____

_____

16.

_____

_____

Name _____   Date _____

THOMAS EDISON'S NEWSPAPER

Do you know the name Thomas Edison? Edison made the first light bulb. Did you know Edison made his own newspaper? He made his newspaper when he was only 15 years old.

Edison was a newspaper boy during the War Between the States. He sold the paper to people riding on a train. The people wanted to know about the war. By the time the newspaper got to the train, the news was old. Edison wanted to get news to the people faster.

First, Edison got an old printing press. He put it on the train. Edison got off the train when it stopped. Then he talked to people who knew about the war.

Next, Edison printed his own newspaper on the train. He wrote about the war. Edison also wrote about the men who worked on the train.

People liked Edison's newspaper. At first he made 100 papers. Soon he was making 300 newspapers.

Today we think about Thomas Edison and his light bulb. Maybe we should also think of him as the boy with his own newspaper.

QUESTIONS FOR THOMAS EDISON'S NEWSPAPER

1. Who made the first light bulb?

   _____

   _____

2. How old was Thomas Edison when he made his newspaper?

   _____

   _____

3. Where did Edison sell his newspapers?

   _____

   _____

4. Where did Edison print his newspaper?

   _____

   _____

5. What was the <u>first</u> thing Edison did to make his newspaper?

   _____

   _____

6. What was the <u>next</u> thing Edison did to make his newspaper?

   _____

   _____

7. What one word best tells about Thomas Edison?

   _____

   _____

8. Why did people like Edison's newspaper?

   _____

   _____

9. Will people always want a newspaper like Edison's on a train? Why do you think so?

_____

_____

10. Why did Edison want to get the news to the people fast?

_____

_____

11. Write a name for the story. Use only a few words.

_____

_____

12. How are Edison's newspaper and today's newspaper alike? How are they not alike?

_____

_____

13. Tell how Edison made his newspaper. Use as few words as you can.

_____

_____

14. Did Edison's paper help the people on the train? Why do you think so?

_____

_____

15. The story said, "People liked Edison's newspaper." Is this a fact? How do you know?

_____

_____

16.

_____

_____

Name _____   Date _____

SEQUOYAH AND THE CHEROKEE ALPHABET

For many years, the Cherokee could not write. They did not know about letters. The Cherokee could not write to their friends. They could not read stories. If a Cherokee child wanted to hear a story, someone had to tell it.

One day a Cherokee man named Sequoyah saw white people writing. He called this writing "talking leaves." Sequoyah wanted to make a Cherokee alphabet.

Sequoyah had to make up his letters. The English letters did not work for Cherokee. Sequoyah worked for almost 10 years. He made 86 Cherokee letters. Each letter stood for a part of a word. Sequoyah was the first person to make a new alphabet by himself.

The new Cherokee letters were easy to learn. Most Cherokees learned to read and write in only a few days.

For the first time, the Cherokee had a newspaper. They called it the Cherokee Phoenix. Cherokee children could now read a story without finding someone to tell it.

D	R	T	ᘛ	Ꝋ	i
SO	Iʔ	y	A	J	E
ŧ	P	A	ŧ	Γ	b
W	δ	ᖯ	G	M	�
ᵞ	Ꝋ	H	ᑕ	y	
Θ	Λ	h	Z	ᑫ	Ꝋ
I	ω	P	V	ᘐ	E
Uꝋ	4	b	ᵼ	ᵷ	R
LW	SL	ᒪ	V	S	ᑕ
88	L	C	ᵼ	ᵽ	P
C	V	ᖾ	K	J	C
G	ᶭ	Ꝋ	ᵴ	ᶘ	6
ᶲ	B	ᖾ	ᵞ	G	B

QUESTIONS FOR SEQUOYAH AND THE CHEROKEE ALPHABET

1. Name the man who made the Cherokee alphabet.

   _____

   _____

2. How many years did Sequoyah work on his letters?

   _____

   _____

3. How long did it take most Cherokees to learn to read and write?

   _____

   _____

4. What was the name of the Cherokee newspaper?

   _____

   _____

5. How did the Cherokee children hear a story before Sequoyah made his alphabet?

   _____

   _____

6. What could the Cherokee people do after Sequoyah made his alphabet?

   _____

   _____

7. What one word best tells about Sequoyah?

   _____

   _____

8. Was Cherokee life better after Sequoyah made his alphabet? Why do you think so?

   _____

   _____

9. Will the Cherokee always use Sequoyah's alphabet? Why do you think so?

_____

_____

10. Why did Sequoyah make a Cherokee alphabet?

_____

_____

11. Write a name for the story. Use as few words as you can.

_____

_____

12. How are Sequoyah's Cherokee letters and English letters alike? How are they not alike?

_____

_____

13. Tell how Sequoyah made his alphabet. Use as few words as you can.

_____

_____

14. How did Sequoyah's alphabet change the lives of his people?

_____

_____

15. The story said, "Sequoyah was the first person to make a new alphabet by himself." Is this a fact? How do you know?

_____

_____

16.

_____

_____

PIÑATAS

Have you been to a party and played with a piñata? Some piñatas are paper bulls filled with candy. Children hit the bull with sticks. The bull breaks and the children run for the falling candy.

The paper bull was a piñata. Piñatas are very old toys.

In Spain, children played with piñatas at Christmas. The Christmas piñata looked like a star. The star had three points. They said each point was one of the Three Wise Men who visited Jesus. The candies in each point were like the gifts the Three Wise Men took to Jesus.

When people from Spain came to Mexico they brought piñatas. The people of Mexico liked the toys. They made them for their children.

The children of Mexico have played with piñatas for many years. Today you can find piñata animals, people, and stars.

You can play with a piñata, too. First, cover your eyes and hold a stick. Next, turn around three times. Last, hit the piñata three times. When it breaks, everyone shares the candy that falls from Mexico's piñata.

QUESTIONS FOR PIÑATAS

1. What did the piñata of Spain look like?

   _____

   _____

? What was inside the points of the star piñata?

   _____

   _____

3. Where did the people of Spain take their piñatas?

   _____

   _____

4. For whom did the people of Mexico make their piñatas?

   _____

   _____

5. What is the first thing you do when you play with a piñata?

   _____

   _____

6. What is the last thing you do when you play with a piñata?

   _____

   _____

7. Why did the people of Spain play with their piñatas at Christmas?

   _____

   _____

8. Are piñatas hard to break? Why do you think so?

   _____

   _____

9. Will children always like playing with piñatas? Why do you think so?

_____

_____

10. Why do children play with piñatas?

_____

_____

11. Write a title for the story. Use as few words as possible.

_____

_____

12. How are the animal and people piñatas of today like Spain's star piñata? How are they not alike?

_____

_____

13. In your own words, tell how to play with a piñata.

_____

_____

14. How would a party change if someone brought a piñata?

_____

_____

15. The story says, "When people from Spain came to Mexico they brought piñatas." Is this a fact? How can you prove your answer?

_____

_____

16.

_____

_____

Name _____   Date _____